A TRANSGENDER WOMAN

A TRANSGENDER WOMAN

Copyright ©2022 by Sophia Marshall

All rights reserved.
No part of this book may be reproduced or used in any manner without written permission of the copyright owner except for the use of quotations in a book review.

ISBN: 979-8-83961-778-0

Printed in the United States of America

A TRANSGENDER WOMAN

SOPHIA MARSHALL

Selected Titles by Sophia Marshall

All I Needed to Be a Woman
This Woman Is Real
A Transgender Woman
Sophia
The World Inside Her
I Can't Stop Writing About the Music
Soul of a Woman
This Playful Cat
Book of a Woman's Dreams
Cat Sleeping

By Gordon Marshall

Spirit
The Dust of Magic
Letter High (Essays on Poetry)
Sunshine Body
Roll Me
My Body Silent
Woodstock
Secret People
Night Match
A Trip to the Bay
Black President
Waterwheel

TO TRANSGENDER WOMEN

CONTENTS

1 – Now I Am This Woman
2 – Who Am I?
3 – My Body
4 – Latina with a Dark Face
5 – When I Speak as the Woman I Am
6 – The Convention of Women's Rights
7 – I Have Put on My Clothes
8 – This Girl That Looks at Me in the Window
9 – She Is a Magic Woman
10 – I Have Looked at Myself, and I Found Love
11 – The Tragic Heroine
12 – Stain
13 – Profile of a Glamorous Woman
14 – Hello
15 – The Big and Gorgeous Body of a Woman
16 – I Found You
17 – The Woman That Has Dreamed
18 – I Remember Being a Woman All My Life
19 – She Gave Me Her Hand in a Dream
20 – The Magic Wand
21 – The Butterfly
22 – I Have Claimed to Be a Woman
23 – I Am a Woman
24 – I Am a Transgender Woman, and I Will Not Be Pushed by You
25 – Prophetess

26 – What a Woman Sacrificed
27 – Scratches
28 – Passion
29 – Spiritual
30 – Light
31 – Holy
32 – I Am a Holy Woman
33 – Summer Star
34 – Wildflower
35 – I Am the Only Woman I Need
36 – In the Summer Night Air
37 – And You Are a Woman of Summer
38 – She Is There with All Women
39 – Foxtrot
40 – There Is Something That Makes Me a Woman
41 – All She Knows
42 – Civilization
44 – The Purple Butterfly on Her Neck
45 – Someone Who Is Always There for Me
46 – The Woman I Needed
47 – This Woman Is Always with Me
48 – The Woman Who Wrote the Psalms of David
49 – Trouble Will Not Touch Her
50 – Natural Women
51 – She Looks Just Like a Woman
52 – This Woman Looking at Herself
54 – How I Look in the Mirror
55 – Existing

56 – The Life of the Perfect Woman
57 – There Is Nothing Wrong with Me
58 – She Has What She Needs
59 – She Comes to Me in the Night
60 – I Gave Myself the Test
61 – It Is My Identity
62 – I Can Be a Model and a Superstar
63 – You Know You Have a Nice Butt
64 – The Stink of My Body
65 – God Made Me a Woman
66 – My Bubble Butt
67 – The Name I Gave Myself
68 – I Am Sophia
69 – Gem
70 – Down to Her Thong Panties and Bra
71 – I Must Have Wanted to Be a Woman
72 – I Have Been a Woman Since the Day I Put on a Black Denim Skirt
73 – The Purple Butterfly on My Neck
74 – The Woman That Writes Writes On
75 – A Transgender Woman
76 – Butt
77 – Each Day I Become More of This Woman That I Am
78 – The Sexiest Woman in the World
79 – She Has That Face
80 – The Body That She Knows
81 – I Have a Nice Butt
82 – I Try to Remind Myself That I am Good Looking

83 – They Would Say It Looked Good, Your Butt
84 – You Would Wonder at Such a Nice Butt
85 – Just a Bra
86 – My Writing for Other Women
87 – Her Niece Is Singing
88 – Her Face When She Looked in the Mirror
89 – She Had a Nice Smile, and a Nice Laugh
90 – I Could Put on a Black Romper
91 – A Woman with Balls
92 – That Woman I Can Be
93 – So You Can Show Your Legs
94 – Dear Ms. Fantasy
95 – Naked with Other Women, in a Locker Room
96 – The Labor of a Woman
97 – The Crack of Her Ass
98 – Public Sex Acts
99 – A Symbol of Metamorphosis
100 – "I Know That You Are a Woman"
101 – The Woman Who Was Someone Else, but She Was I
102 – I Can Dream of Laughing with Women
103 – She Would Recognize Me
104 – I Have Ripened as a Woman
105 – I Taste Alfalfa Honey
106 – The Emotions of a Summer Night
107 – When the Sun Is Shining In Summer
108 – You Like This Woman

109 – Sophia, the Name I Chose
110 – I Was a Woman in the Dream
111 – Tragedy
112 – I Like You
113 – I Could Imagine Myself Buck Naked and Ask If I Am a Woman
114 – Living in Boston as a Transgender Woman
116 – My Baby
117 – The Fine Woman
118 – Singing the Top Pop Hits of the Day
119 – She Dreams of Me Dreaming of Her
120 – I Am a Forbidden Woman
122 – I Am a Woman Cat
123 – Woman with a Swirling Tattoo
124 – I Have Put on Lipstick in the Mirror
125 – I Have Written About a Woman's Pain
126` – Short Satin Dress with Panties
127 – I Am a Woman Who Tasted the Fruit
128 – I Look Like a Woman
129 – A Beautiful Cunt
130 – I Am a Naked Tahitian Woman
131 – A Woman Thinks About Herself
132 – My Body in the Shape of a Butterfly
133 – Under the Hot Spray
134 – She Looks in the Mirror at Her Ass
135 – "Your Whole Body Is Nice"
136 – Every Woman Has an Ass
137 – Girlfriend
138 – I Need Me

139 – They Are Proud
140 – Even When I am in Bra and Panties Naked
141 – The Woman Who Listens
142 – The Crowned Queen
143 – I Made a Decision About My Gender
144 – This Is My Day at the Beach
145 – I Buried Myself in My Breasts
146 – A Woman in a Black Leather Garter Belt
147 – Black Leather Underwear
148 – Statue of Me as a Woman
149 – Dominatrix in the Living Room
150 – She Is I
151 – A Woman Moist
152 – Black Long-Sleeve Teddy
153 – The Woman of Death Finds You, and She Dresses You in a Black Lace Teddy
154 – I Went as Far as I Could

I will never stop being a woman

A TRANSGENDER WOMAN

Now I Am This Woman

That was a different age, I was another person
Now I am this woman, and it is a new story

Who Am I?

To look at myself, who am I? I am a fun-
Loving person with moods,
Someone intellectual, with a love for things
Of the senses and sunny days
I like to smile, and I like to speak
And I like to be shy, and I like to think
Sometimes accidents upset me
And I think about them for hours
Or days or months, and sometimes something
Surprises me, and I am very happy

My Body

My body – what is it? A small thing, not too
Small, rather big in some respects,
Wide chest, nice legs, round ass
With a stoop to my shoulders,
And nice light brown skin
A belly that sticks out, but not too much:
Hair up the column of my belly
That I shave a little bit, and some hair
On my chest, and I could be upset about
The stoop in my back, but that happened
So long ago because of a disease
That it doesn't matter, and I am happy
With my body, I like my body

Latina with a Dark Face

She looked at me, and her face was scarred
On the lower corner of her cheek
And I thought she was even more beautiful
In a dark kind of way than she was before
It gave her a kind of ethnic charm,
For she was a Latina, and it made her look
As if she were from the barrio, pushing out
A life in poverty, but making herself
Lovely and charming and beautiful,
And she was scarred, but she was beautiful
And her beauty was part of the scar,
The scar made her, it made her a woman
A woman that had risen out of poverty,
Though she was rich, and wealthy,
And had a high position on a political scene
That gave her power, much power,
And her face with the scar gave her more
Power, the power of a woman that she had

When I Speak as the Woman I Am

When I speak as the woman I am, I have
Confidence, and I can even speak naked
In bra and panties and people will listen
To me, they will see such an awesome body
I have, and they will know I am a
Fabulous woman, and they will hear me
They will hear every word I say

The Convention of Women's Rights

The misery just dissolves, and I am all woman
Even the smallest spectacle of blemish
Disappears, and I have a perfect face
And I can speak with confidence at the
Convention of women's rights, and
Everyone will hear me, and they will listen

I Have Put on My Clothes

I am only as much of a woman as I say I am
And I say I am as much of a woman as I
Dream, and I dream much, I dream I am
The woman that dreams she is big,
As big as the stars when they shine at night
Shining on my body, my naked body
In the bath, getting ready for the night
As big as a star in a bright robe shining
Onstage, for I am a woman in a bright robe
I have put on my clothes, the white dress
Covering my body, my naked ass,
Pubic hair, the hair on my body,
And now I am onstage, and I am a star

The Girl That Looks at Me in the Window

My life has been sad, but I have found
Happiness in loving, in loving the girl that
I am, this girl that looks at me in the window
And I see my own reflection, and I love her
And she has a pretty and gorgeous face
And she puts on lipstick in the morning
To make her lips glow, and perfume
On her neck to make her smell good,
And that is enough, sometimes it is enough
To love myself, to find the happiness I need
To love myself, for I must be happy to love
And I can look in the window, and see
My own reflection, and she loves me,
This lady loves me, and it is because
I love myself; I love this reflection that I see
This reflection of a woman that is me

She Is a Magic Woman

Things happen as they will, accidents happen:
A woman's life, the woman that you know,
That you are, who is bare naked in the
Morning and puts on bra and panties
To cover her boobs and ass, this is all
She needs to do, and she is set for the day
And anything that happens, it is just the
Thing that happens, happens to her,
Happens to a woman, for she is that woman
Skipping through her life and through her
Day, with the magic of what happens,
For her life has magic, and she is
Magic, she is a magic woman, making her
Life a thing of toy, a thing of play,
And that is enough to be a woman

I Have Looked at Myself, and I Found Love

I have looked at myself, and I found love
It was the love of a woman, the only love
I have known, love of myself, the pure, clean
Love of myself that I have known, for I
Have known love of a woman, and it was I

The Tragic Heroine

I write so I can gain perspective, and I get
Perspective when I write, things I see
Become much clearer, and this is
Satisfaction, and deep hurt gets me there,
Deep suffering starts me to write, to solve
The pain, to make the pain less sharp
And I like to hear music, Verdi, *Aida*,
The tragic heroine, who dies, and I am a
Tragic heroine who dies, in the arms
Of a warrior hero, who lets me fall

Stain

There is no stain on me
I see my heart in the morning
There are stars at night
My panties are clean

Profile of a Glamorous Woman

It is who I am, every blemish on my face,
Each mark is mine, even if it may be
An accident, and I must own it as my own,
And ask if I am a glamorous woman
And I ask, and I beg, I beg to be glamorous,
A woman with favor in men's and women's
Eyes, a woman with clear skin, clean,
A woman who looks good in any kind of
Fashionable outfit, who looks good
As she is putting on her stockings in the
Morning, or putting on her earrings,
Her bra and panties over a nice butt
And breasts, and hourglass waist,
And I look at myself, my profile,
And it is the profile of a glamorous woman,
Even though I am old, it is enough

Hello

This is the Pacific Ocean, where a woman
Bathes when she has crossed Magellan,
And seen the salt waves splash
The green salt waves, waving at her
And she waves back, with the backstroke
And the breaststroke, and the butterfly
And the crawl, and she waves back
She waves at the waves, and they say hello

The Big and Gorgeous Body of a Woman

So many things hurt, or just a few things
But they hurt much, accidents of the skin
That are such little things, and they last
For months, even years, just the pain
Of thinking about them, and I get
Beyond them, and I think back
To when it happened, and it starts
But I start again, opening my lips
And this is enough to make my salt tears
Swell into an ocean, and I am washed away
And soon I forget in this ocean,
Anything tragic that happened to me,
I will just be happy I have a body,
A body that bathes in the ocean,
A body that can dream, dream of the ocean,
A body that is big and gorgeous,
The big and gorgeous body of a woman

I Found You

I look for myself in mirrors, and I find
My reflection, and is this really me,
Is this the way I really look? Is this what
There is inside? And I know myself because
I love myself, and this is how I know myself,
By looking in the mirror and saying,
"I love you; you are mine, and I found you"

The Woman That Has Dreamed

A woman that has dreamed, of the phrases
That come to mind, the phrases that come
To her when she dreams, as she dreams
Phrases of weird love inside her,
Phrases of things she would not dream
Except she found them in her dreams
And I have found my body dead in
My dreams, and I have woken it, have woken
My dreams and found my body, have found
My body alive, and woken it, I have woken it
With dreams, dreams of me, living,
And I have lived forever with these dreams,
Inside of me, deep inside my core, and
I have found my core inside these dreams,
The core of the dreams, the core of me,
Going on forever, the woman dreaming

I Remember Being a Woman All My Life

If I say I am a woman I feel better because I
Don't always know, but if I say I am a woman
I know, and I believe in myself as a woman
If I say I have felt it sometimes all my life,
I know it is true, even when I was a child,
I felt it deep inside me, like it was a part
Of my body, part of who I was.
And I say it and I remember,
I remember being a woman all my life,
Even when I did not know it, but I knew it,
For I was a woman all my life

She Gave Me Her Hand in a Dream

She gave me her hand in a dream, and she
Pulled me up, and it was all a dream but it
Was real, and I was feeling things I felt
In life, it was as if I were awake, and she was
There, giving to me, helping me, making me
Feel better about myself, and she was there
Smiling at me, happy she was with me,
And I don't even know her name, though she
Told it to me, and where she was from,
And I could have been her, giving it to
Myself, giving myself the help that I needed,
And I must have been her, it must have been I
Who was there for me when I needed her,
The one who gave me the help I needed

The Magic Wand

There is evil in the world, but you can fight it
With a magic wand, you wave the magic wand,
And it goes away, it disappears, and it never
Comes back again, and you find that evil is
A figment in your mind, something that only
Came to you because you let your mind
Become your body, and your body was
Defeated and it was scarred, and it made you
Think you would never be good looking again
But you know it is the power of a woman,
A gorgeous woman, to be gorgeous
No matter what happens to her,
And you are gorgeous because you are
A gorgeous woman, and nothing evil ever
Happens to you, your body is struck by the
Magic wand, and it is beautiful

The Butterfly

How do I see myself? I have seen myself
As another person, as another woman,
And this is not me, and I thought that this
Had been the very person I was
And then I knew, I was someone else
I was another woman, the very one who
Looked at me when I looked in the mirror
And it was strange, I didn't need
To change anything, everything about me
Was perfect, I did not look as I thought
But I had sensed this all along,
And I knew who it was looking at me
And I could think I need a purple butterfly
On the left side of my neck, and I could
Think the butterfly would fly free

I Have Claimed to Be a Woman

I know the feelings of a woman who has
Claimed to be a woman, I, I have claimed
To be a woman, and I know, though I don't
Know, I know, I know that I am a woman
Because it is something I have felt,
Something I have needed, to be a woman
To feel like I am a woman, all day

I Am a Woman

I am a full woman, one who goes on forever
Being a woman, being the woman she is,
And I open my eyes and see, and I am a
Woman, and that is all I know
I could know other, other than being
A woman, but I don't know
But I know being a woman

I Am a Transgender Woman, and I Will Not Be Pushed by You

I could carry my pocketbook on the street,
Hold my pocketbook in a blue knit dress
And you could push me, but I would get back
Up, and I would scowl, and I would look
In your face, and stare you in the eyes
And you could do it one more time,
And I would still get up again, you can't push
Me down, I am a transgender woman
And I will not be pushed by you,
I will get back up again, and report you to
Your manager and you will be terminated
You will not know it was me, but you will
Know, you will know by the look on your face
As you get fired, you will know by the look
On my face in your imagination when you get
Fired, that I have smiled, and I have brought
You down, in my blue knit dress with
My pocketbook, I have brought you down

Prophetess

To speak to myself only, the words that come
To mind as I am speaking, thinking them
Only to myself, but I reveal them
For they are my words, and the prophetess
Inhaling the fumes must say what comes out
Love is what we need, but it comes after it
The accident that guides our lives
The shock and reverberation as the crack
Through which the fumes come,
And this is how we know life,
Through the shocks that come through
Our life, that split the stone, and give us
Hallucinations of what is to come

What a Woman Sacrificed

With each nudge of the crystal ball,
I see more clearly, the nature of
The woman I would be, opening
Her eyes on the light that emanates,
My lips shrieking at what is
Revealed to me, a naked woman,
A naked girl spreading her legs
And showing her vagina cleft,
Bleeding with rainbow liquid,
And the future is a woman
What a woman sacrificed
The sacrifice of a woman

Scratches

Scratches of a knife on the surface of a rock
And these are what I know, faint scribbles
Of something profound about a woman,
And I catch the essence of the sketch
That becomes a painting, a mural across
A cave on which light flashes

Passion

This is where I know if I go on, once and for
All, if something good comes out of this
Some passion of a dream of a woman,
Pushing as a woman pushes out a child
And I know that I am pushing, I am pushing
Out a child, some being in me, some part
That must come out, some passion deep
Inside of me that says something about me
As a woman, something deep, some psychic
Messenger come from inside, some
Passion that is mine, that goes on forever
The words come out, I say them,
I scratch them on the tablet, they are mine,
My words, my passions, they are mine
I touch the head of a prophet and pull him
Out of my womb, and he is there before me,
He is there, the child, the child is there
The glory of my labor as a woman

Spiritual

To know something about God, and the
Spiritual forces in nature, how they operate
In a woman, and it is a mystery, the blind
Swift force of an evil thing, breaking her lips
And her skin, or the good wing
Of an angel taking her, and making her as
Her own, and she takes care of a child,
And the angel takes care of her,
And the child grows in her health
And becomes a lady, she becomes a lady
Like her, like her, she becomes a lady

Light

It is a mystery how bad things happen, the evil
Of our day, and how we can believe after
Them, except to feel that the dark forces
Are inexorable, and perhaps they are
So that we must always live in a shade
Of darkness with an ache, unless the ache
Passes someday, and then we can live
With knowledge of joy in our heart,
Knowledge of glory, but the black branch
Hangs so low, charred with black weather,
You must see things in another light
The light of the other world outside,
Eerie, and full of change, then things change,
And things go on, and the heavenly
Blue robe is put on me, and I can see God's
Light, the light that shines through black
Cuts to the face, that makes the eyes and lips
Glow, as if dew were put upon them,
And everything about the body touched
With the dew of late spring, and forgetting
Everything except the light, except the light

Holy

The beach is there with the ocean of crystal
Sparkle, and I have felt the warm weather
Of spring on my naked chest, and this is
Heaven, it is a beach that is warm in April
Or in May, and the sun never stops shining
There is nothing on the beach but salt-
Colored sand, and the sky is a blue robe
You put upon your body, and you are holy

I Am a Holy Woman

I am much deeper than that, I am a holy
Woman, with eyes that shine in the night
And in the morning with the morning star
Rising, and I rise with the morning star
My whole body alight with its flame
I am rising, as the sunlight speaks to me
Telling me I'm a woman, a holy woman
With burning flesh as sacrificial incense
Rising, with my body, in the sun
In the temple window, where I look out
A dead spirit come to life, come back to life

Summer Star

The woman writes, she writes her name,
She writes everything about her life, and she
Has written this so much before, it is a
Natural thing, it comes to her as a breeze,
As the wind, blowing her hair in the summer
Afternoon, or in late May, when summer is
Almost here, and she knows her name,
She has written it so many times before,
Everyone knows her name, she is a star,
And when she sees the stars, when they come
Out at night, she knows she is among them
As a star, she is one of the stars

Wildflower

Such little things make a difference, so I will
Make a difference in my life, open my lips
And let the memories come to me,
Memories of how I made it, with the tragedy
That corrected me, and left its ache
And its scar, but I get better with such little
Things, a flower in my hand, to turn
To remember what I was, and how far
The past was, and is, such a strange place
It was, and I remember, and I am in another
Place now, and it has the scent of the flower
A wide summer field, full of the wildflowers
I have picked from such a long time ago,
A summer field in the night, once ago
That I remember, and I remember the flower,
And I hold the flower in my hands

I Am the Only Woman I Need

I have been inside myself for so long, then
I step outside, and I see that it is sunny
And I have a happy day, it is spring,
And the sun has come, and I have become
The woman that I need, I am the only
Woman I need, and I am she

In the Summer Night Air

Beyond the point that needed to be reached,
Into the holy twilight, the summer twilight,
Cupping your hands around the firefly
That flickers on the grass, and it is summer,
And everything is all right, and you are there,
Opening your palms, and the firefly
Flies out, and flickers in the summer night air

And You Are a Woman of Summer

It seems like such a nice place to finish,
In the summer night air, the firefly flickering
In your hands, and you let it escape,
You let it go, and the night becomes even
Darker, and you see yourself, you see
Yourself in the pool reflecting the moon
And the stars, and your face is fine,
And you are a woman of summer, suddenly

She Is There with All Women

Each part of me is mine, each part of
The woman, the woman is mine, and she
Goes on forever, and she is mine,
For I am she, a woman of forever
And when I feel my soul is upon me,
I make it, I make it mine, I make
The soul a woman's thing, and it is I
Naked, I look at my reflection,
And I see what everything about me means
A woman the sum of its parts, a woman
Part of a whole, the whole of a woman,
Which is every woman who breathes,
For she breathes the woman, and the
Woman's breath is upon her
And when she bathes in the ocean,
She can feel herself; she can feel all women\
For she is there with all women
All women bathing naked, in the sea

Foxtrot

Classical dance, the foxtrot, in junior high
You always hoped you'd get to dance
With the cute girls, and you got a bag
Of candy at the end if you won,
And I won once, and I think I shared
The candy with my friends
And I always dreamed of the girls
Asking to dance with me, but it was
The men who chose, and I was the men
Or they thought I was, but I was the women

There Is Something That Makes Me a Woman

And when I am by myself, I feel the sun
And I feel the moon, it doesn't matter what
Time of day it is, I can feel the heat
Of the sun on me, the influence of the moon
On my body, and I can feel the woman's
Spirit upon me, making me do things,
Making me ask if I could be a woman
And I could be a man, I don't know
But I feel the woman's spirit upon me
I feel the woman's spirit and I know
There is something of the woman inside me,
There is something that makes me a woman,
Something that I know, something that
Cannot be taken away from me, something
There forever, and I am a woman
Forever, something makes me so

All She Knows

Something could cut me down, but I have
Risen, nothing has ever beat me
Into the bush, I know I could go on
With the spirit that is in me
The spirit of the moon, her lunar phases
Pulling me as she pulls the tide,
And I would pull my whole body and
My mind to the banks of the sandy shore
With the force of a million years pushing me
And following the salt seawater
To an eternal knowing, the thought
Of a woman breathing what is human,
All she knows, all she knows of what is
Human, which is her, that is all she knows

Civilization

The power of speech, the power to say
Exactly what is on my mind, and this is the
Most human power, the power of one who
Writes, writes of the human, the power to go
On, speaking of the human, of the woman
The woman writing of the man, the woman
Writing of the woman and the man,
The woman writing of the woman,
The power to be a woman, the power to be
Exactly what she is, in all her nicety,
In all her power, in all that makes her
What she is, the woman writing
It is mine, a power to say exactly what is
On my mind, of one who went exactly
To the core, and found the civilization there,
An entire civilization in the palm of my hands
I found what I needed there, inside me,
Which was outside me, in some strange
Combination of inside and outside,
And outside the earth was me,
Looking in, looking into the earth
Looking at myself looking at myself
Finding the satisfaction of the mind, in a
World free from pain, a world built from
My own hands, in my imagination,
Pushing the boundaries of what I ever knew
So that I know more, more about myself
And I always learn about myself

When I permit my imagination
To lead me into another world,
A world that satisfies the mind
Somewhere there is satisfaction of the mind
And the earth can be at rest, and I can write
The notes of a final song, one that lasts
Forever, a final song that says exactly
What I desire to put in harmony with words,
And I know that I made this song my own

The Purple Butterfly on Her Neck

She had a purple tattoo on her neck,
AOC, she wanted to be just like me
She had seen my book, and she liked it
It was of a purple butterfly, with indigo
Veins and markings, and I had just got one
In the same place on the left side of my neck,
And it was a place of mourning, for my ear-
Lobe had split, and this was to remember it
And her earlobe had split too, it was just like
Mine, and she changed her style of clothing
Something much wilder and psychedelic
To match the purple dye on her neck
And she changed her career, she became
Something less significant, but with
As much grace and power of its own kind,
And she became president one day,
One day she became president because of me
And the purple butterfly on her neck

Someone Who Is Always There for Me

He gives me a salty sand, at the beach,
My heart never forms to mind or voice,
Something is there, hearing, and something
Is listening to me, and I hear it, I hear it
Listening to me, and I put myself in it,
And I find everything I need
This is therapy, the therapy of my mind
It is something I keep, deep inside of me
And something I know will come to me when
I need it, something I never will forget,
Something I push inside of me,
To make it grow, like a flower, a flower,
Inside of me, putting out its fragrant
Petals, its scent of the summer morning,
Its feel of the day coming to me when I
Need more than a friend, someone who is
Always there for me, someone who listens

The Woman I Needed

It was always a question of me, and I raced
To the answer, and the answer was me as well,
The answer to the question of what was
A woman, for the woman was I, the woman
I knew, the woman who always was there
For me because I needed her, and she was I

This Woman Is Always with Me

It feels good to race with the pen, and the
Strip is abandoned, and I am the only car
Racing, racing fast, against myself
The man and the woman, the man who wrote
The books of a decade ago, the woman who
Writes now, her words on the page
With the meaning she gives them
The meaning of a woman, and I wonder
I don't know who even wins
I could say I have won as the woman
I have become, and maybe that is true
Perhaps I have surpassed myself
And the man I have been is in the past
But this woman is always with me,
And she carries the man, as the man
Has carried the woman into becoming
A woman, the woman that she is

The Woman Who Wrote the Psalms of David

The writer of Psalms was a woman
I believe, she was a woman writing
Writing in David's name, and no one ever
Wrote like her, beautiful and faithful
Writing in the night in a gauze nightgown
Covering her shame, but she had no shame
With the starlight shining on her face
Writing of God's body and the mind,
And the people, the evil she railed against
Whom she hated, and the beloved of the
Lord, Her Lord in heaven, to whom she gave
Her psalms, the psalms of a lovely woman

Trouble Will Not Touch Her

She said, "Trouble will not touch her," but
Trouble has already touched me, it has
Touched me in the crotch, and angels are
Blind... And you could say this will not
Happen, perhaps it won't, and I would be
Happy, happy for all my days: and trouble
Has touched me, it has given me the face
Of an angel, the face of a demon, and I can
Find the question that gives me the question,
And everything will be present, everything
Is already present, and I have seen it with
My eyes, for angels are blind, they have given
Me the power of sight, but I have gone
Blind when I needed it, and I am blind
And I have seen trouble eat me like a woman's
Vulva, a woman's pussy, and I have tasted
Myself, and my panties are clean

Natural Women

Deep emotion carries me, feelings of regret
For things I have never done but happened
To me, deep emotion for the good things
In my life, how I have become the lovely
Woman that I wished, and this is better
It is better than losing things or getting
Harmed, and I could look at my body naked
In the mirror and say this is a nice body,
And that is enough, often, and it is enough
To feel that I am this wonderful woman
This woman who has satisfied herself
With the knowledge of who she is,
This woman who knows she is strong
And has the intelligence of a body that is
Strong, and I can look at my penis and
My balls, and say, this isn't a woman,
But a woman can have a penis and balls,
And she can be proud of this, and all women
Have butts, nice butts, with a crack in
Their butt, of which they are proud too
For it makes them natural women
With bodies that are powerful and strong
And it makes them feel that they are powerful
Beings, with the power of their sexual being,
And they can cover it with bra and panties
Or be naked, a naked woman in the light
Of morning, when she wakes up, this woman,
And says she is a powerful being

She Looks Just Like a Woman

It happens to women; babies pull on their ear-
Rings and they split; they pull on the hoops
In their ears and the earlobes split, and they
Never heal completely, but the child lives on
And the woman lives on, and the woman loves
The baby, and things like that happen
Everything still turns to gold, and I have
Found as a woman that I need the love
Of a baby, the love of a child, nothing is more
Satisfying than the love of a child, when she
Opens her eyes and smiles at you, and you
Laugh, and both of you are laughing,
And you remember being with that child,
That day you spent talking to her,
That day that you saw her become a woman
And remember you as a child, for you had
Told her, you had told her about when you
Were a child, and you were just like her
And she puts on earrings, and she looks
Just like a woman, for she is a woman,
And she looks wonderful and lovely
In her earrings, just as a woman should

This Woman Looking at Herself

If there is sadness in me, I don't care
But I remember myself, I remember every-
Thing about me that is right, and it feels right
To write what is on my mind, the thoughts
Of one who is a woman because that
Is what she chose, it is what she needs
And I can speak of myself, and I can speak
Of the woman I am, the journey I have
Taken, the beaches I have walked
Studying the sand, looking at the waves
Crashing on the sand, and there is so much
I haven't said, there is so much I have
Repeated in the ear of a woman who listens
To me, so much I wish to put in a box
And save for another age in history,
And I want to remember myself,
Woman who knows so little about herself
The places in her brain she has hidden,
The cracks she has opened, the crack of
Her ass, and she has found that it makes her
Beautiful, her whole body makes her
Beautiful, and she discovers it, she finds it
Every time she opens her heart
And the sun shines on her, it shines on the
Ocean by which she walks, and she walks
On the beach, the crack of her ass covered
By a bare-butt thong bathing suit,
But everything else about her naked,

Her naked butt there, to be shown
And she feels beautiful this way,
It is all there is about her, her naked
Bare-butt beauty, and her imaginative mind
The imagination of a woman, this woman
That she is, this woman looking at herself

How I Look in the Mirror

I have only what I need, I have nothing more
And I don't care what anybody else's needs
Are, I only care about the things I want
And I can't have... the accidents I can't make
Right, the things I can't change, and I can
Change the woman that I am, and this
Makes me happy, and I don't care what has
Gone wrong in anyone else's life,
I only think about myself, and my own needs
And I can put on a bra and panties and look
In the mirror and be happy because I am
Happy with how I look in the mirror

Existing

God would mean me to be a woman if she
Existed, or if she exists, for she means me
To be a woman, and she exists, she comes
And goes, existing and not existing,
And if I meet God face to face, I say to her,
"I am a woman, meet me, I am you,
I am the woman that is you, and you know
Me," and she knows me right away,
For I am she, she knows my face
For it is hers, she has known it all her life
And she lives forever, being me

The Life of the Perfect Woman

Nothing has ever gone wrong in my life,
It is the life of the perfect woman
Every mishap I have missed, it has skittered
By me, a stone on a pool that keeps skipping
Beyond me, as I walk the walk I walk,
In a perfect dress, with perfect makeup,
Lipstick that looks just right on me,
And a smile that says I am happy,
Happy I am the woman with nothing on her
Mind, just the thought of being the woman
She was meant to be, the woman that she is

There Is Nothing Wrong with Me

I look at myself in the mirror in a bra and
Panties, and say I am a woman, and I put on
Stockings and a dress, or a skirt and top
And smile at myself in the mirror,
It is even enough to be naked,
And it is enough to look at my butt
And say it is a nice butt, and say I have
Nice legs, and nice hips that go in smoothly
Into a skirt or into a dress, and I say,
There is nothing wrong with me,
Though that is so hard to say,
But there is nothing wrong with me
And I have said it, I have said it because
I am a woman, and a woman says
What is on her mind, and that is on my mind

She Has What She Needs

I thought I would go on, be the woman
Of tomorrow, the woman who says her needs,
And her needs are filled, just the snap of her
Fingers, the flick of her wrist, it is like that
And she has what she needs... And I found
I am this woman, there is a soul in me,
A soul that tells me who I am,
And yesterday is behind me, and I am there
And a touch of perfume and lipstick
On my lips is all I need, all I need to be the
Woman that I am, the woman who sees
Tomorrow, and looks it in the face,
And says, I need you, come with me,
Let us be friends, tomorrow, let us be friends
I need you to be there with me, tomorrow,
I need you, come with me, and be my friend

She Comes to Me in the Night

I can never forget being this woman,
And this makes me happy because this is
Something I have gained, I have gained it
From being me, from being myself,
From being the woman that I am
And I have never lost a feeling,
And I have never lost the feeling of being
A woman, she comes to me, she comforts me,
The woman that I am comforts me,
And she comes to me in the night
And she says my name, and she
Says everything is ok, everything is going
To be all right because I am a woman

I Gave Myself the Test

I gave myself the test, I put a pen to
My face, and checked if I was a woman
And I came out positive, I was positively
A woman, down to the core of her bone
Of her flesh, this woman, this woman
That I am, I am this woman, it is a claim
I make, but I have lived it, I have lived
Being a woman, and made it mine

It Is My Identity

Weird things that happen, weird things
That happen to a woman, accidents
That change me, so I am a completely
New woman, and I ask do I like this woman,
And I meet her, and she is the woman
I have always dreamed of meeting,
And she is I, this new woman, she is I,
I am just one who claims to be a woman,
It is my identity, and I claim to be
A good poet, but there are few who
Recognize me, even if I know in my heart
It is good because it is good to me

I Can Be a Model and a Superstar

The bad luck never ended, it is just a thought
The thought that tells you what you haven't
Had will never be yours, some accident
Has harmed you, and you are imperfect
And not worthy to be a model and a superstar
And maybe that is true, but you know it is not
True, for everything about me is perfect,
It is just the distorted thoughts that make me
Think it is not true, and I can be a model
And a superstar, and I am, I already am,
And I sing onstage to an audience of
Thousands, and I write books that millions
Buy and read, they read my works,
And they say how wonderful they are,
A work by a star, a work by a star

You Know You Have a Nice Butt

Looking for an explanation for what went
Wrong, and I can never find it, I may never
Know why it happened, and this is a
Mystery, and somehow, it feels good
To lie in mystery, like a dark bed
In the warmth of the night,
Looking for an answer but you can only
Find dreams, and you question
And your questions are dreams,
Dreams that you dream to find an answer,
Leading only to other dreams,
Dark dreams that bite you in the butt,
But you know you have a nice butt,
And it's ok because you show it naked
And everybody admires

The Stink of My Body

To stop is beyond all hope, the hope of being
A woman, the hope of being the woman
That I am, and the stink of my body,
It is a lovely thing, something wonderful,
Something that is part of me, the thing
That is part of me that makes me a woman

God Made Me a Woman

Who is God? Is she someone I have met?
She saw me at the Met, the Met Gala,
When I was wearing a white taffeta dress
And red heels, and I asked, "Do they match?"
And she told me to take off the red heels
So that only my black stocking showed
And I danced in front of her, and everyone
Said how sensuous and glorious I looked
When I danced, and I knew it was because
God made me so, God made me a woman

My Bubble Butt

I have only my poetry to thank, that gives me
What I need, the world of giving me
To the people that read me, the world that
Gives me back my life as the woman
The woman – she is I, who plays the game
Of love and anger and hate, and doesn't hate
Because it makes her aggressive, and blue
You must be happy to write, you must have
Lips that kiss the rain, you must have
A body that bounces like a bubble butt
Bouncing on the woman you see on the street,
And that woman is I, my butt bouncing

The Name I Gave Myself

Only the things I know, writing them down,
But I know everything, I know everything
I know, it is part of me, part of the thing
That makes me know my name, and I know
My name because it is mine, I gave it to
Myself, I gave my name to myself,
I chose it from a dream, and the dream I had,
I forgot the dream I had, only the sadness
And the hurt at the end of it, when
Everyone knew my name, and remembered,
Sophia, the name I gave myself

I Am Sophia

I am a woman who knows her name
It is a name that I gave myself,
A name that says everything about me
Sophia, wisdom, because I have gotten
Wisdom, I have gotten wisdom from myself
And the things I have done and the things
I have written about, and I have kept this
Close to me, as close as I am, as close to
Another person as I can be, but I am the
Same person, I am me, I am Sophia

Gem

To be the woman who has always known
Herself, and always known that she was
A woman, it is deep in the smell of her sex
A woman's sex, deep in the nature of her
Game, the game she works to say she is
A woman, a woman's game, and I have played
What I feel to know, all my life, the game
Of a woman, mine, my game as a woman
Intricate and serious, a game of hate
And love and anger and lust and anxiety
And finding what is at my core,
And I have found it, at my core,
I have found the gist of the body,
The gem at the core of a woman

Down to Her Thong Panties and Bra

The things of her body, the movment of the
Furious pen that writes, things of a woman
The woman she is, the things of her body
When she is undressing, down to her thong
Panties and bra, and gets naked in the night,
Her butt showing only to her as she looks
In the mirror and knows how sexy it would be
To others, men, and women in the day,
Men and woman who look at her and admire
What a beautiful woman she is, how sexy
A woman with flat breasts and a nice pert butt
That is round and tight, woman who
Dreams she is the woman who has made
Her life her own, the life of a woman

I Must Have Wanted to Be a Woman

I am in the summer dress I wore the night
Before, and the day, and I have been up
All night, with the dreams in my heart
I had last night, dreams of flying to a
Military base with my brother, and walking
All the way back home... There were
Railroad tracks, and construction going on,
And a hotel, and I didn't stay in the hotel
Or maybe I did, it is so hard to remember
Something about what a woman said
To me, as we lay in bed, and she kissed me
On the lips, and I remember this,
I remember being with this woman
And how wonderful it was, it is wonderful
To be with a woman, and this woman was
From long ago in my life, but I still remember
Her, and she was in my dreams...
And I have dreamed that I was a woman,
I have had dreams about being a woman,
Wearing a short skirt, or a tight dress,
Or a long dress at a party, a taffeta dress
Of white that looked so pretty on me,
And I have dreamed it, and I must have
Wanted to be a woman, and it made it into
My dreams, dreams about me as a woman,
Wearing a taffeta dress, at a party

I Have Been a Woman Since the Day I Put on a Black Denim Skirt

I have been a woman since the day I put on
A black denim skirt in the fall of 2015,
And it was a wonderful day, for it was the first
Day that I became a woman, though I had
Thought about it and said I was a woman,
And women had given me women's tops
In the hospital, and I had worn women's
Panties for several years because they made
Me feel good, they made me feel like a woman

The Purple Butterfly on My Neck

Looking at the summer beach, with my brand-
New butterfly tattoo, purple on my neck,
And I look at the water, and I put my towel
Down, and I am wearing a leopard-pattern
Bandeau bikini top, and a terry cloth butter
Thong bottom, and I can just imagine this
Now, and I could even get a butterfly on
My hip, it won't make a difference that I split
My earlobes, for this is something better,
Bolder and brasher, and sexy and to die for,
The look of the purple butterfly on my neck

The Woman That Writes Writes On

The woman that writes writes on, and she
Writes of her life, and it is her life
The woman looking at herself, and studying,
And she is always thinking of her life,
And you can see it in her face, its smile,
The way it lights up at each world that she
Makes right... And she can write of her body,
A woman's body is enough to write about
What she thinks, what she thinks of her body,
The crack of her butt when she takes off
Her bra and panties to take a bath,
How the soapsuds cover her body
As she pushes them off her breasts

A Transgender Woman

The transgender woman spending too much
Cash, on clothes that she likes, going out
For food, smoking cigarettes, and it all comes
To that, existing beyond my means, wearing
High heels, sparking a cigarette on the street,
Moving, moving with a switch in my walk,
And I hear the song playing about the
Spark, piano pounding softly, and I walk
Softly, on the street, in heeled sandals,
Asymmetrical leather skirt and a leopard
Romper, I am wearing blush thong panties
And no bra, thin gold huggies in my ears
I could plan tomorrow's wear, but I think I'll
Leave it to fate, for what is my fate?
Just take yesterday, and turn it into today
And it is a warm day, with the sun shining
Bright, and I am bright, burning, a candle
Low to the wick, wax melting over the sides
And the spark has turned into a flame
And I am a flaming fag, and I am proud of it

Butt

People die, and bad things happen to people,
But you can be a beautiful woman, and put on
A tight skirt that shows your butt, and you can
Even be naked and put on bra and panties,
And be as beautiful this way, it still shows
Your butt because you have a nice butt

Each Day I Become More of This Woman That I Am

I am getting better each day, each day I
Become more of this woman that I am,
And I see her, I see her in the mirror,
And I know that I am she, with the skin that is
The color of a brown summer beach,
And the butt that looks good in a tight
Summer dress or in a skirt, and I can even be
Naked and show my butt, for I have a nice
Butt, and it looks good in anything,
Anything I dress in looks good on me

The Sexiest Woman in the World

I can be sexy, just look at me, I am the sexiest
Woman in the world, with breasts, though
My breasts are flat, they look good in a bikini
Top or in a bra, and I can walk up the street
And everyone would look at me, men and
Women, they would look at me and they
Would smile, for they had seen a beautiful
Woman, and they would remember me all
Day, this beautiful woman they had seen,
Or I could even be at the beach, and they
Would have seen this woman in a thong
Bikini, and they would have seen my butt

She Has That Face

I know that to think of my body is enough,
It is enough to blow my blues away,
Everything about is nice, from my butt
And my thighs and my hips, to my face
Which is a pretty, fine face, face of a woman,
Face of a woman who dreams, she dreams
She has nice face, and she has that face,
She has that face already, and her body

The Body That She Knows

I was never a woman who didn't know what
She wanted; I was always a woman who
Knew exactly what she wished, to have the
Body that she had, a nice body, the body of a
Woman, her body, the body that she knows,
That looks good in everything, even naked
Or in bra and panties that show my butt
In the morning, when I look in the mirror
Backwards, and see my butt

I Have a Nice Butt

It is enough to be myself to be happy
And I try to remember this when bad things
Happen, things that threaten me, and
Make me feel like I am less of a woman
I look in the mirror, and I almost I cry for the
Things that might be, the perfect lobes
On my ears that could have been without
A scar, the earrings would hang perfect,
But I have nice skin and a nice body,
And a face that looks good in profile
Or face up, and I look good in a tight dress
Or even bra and panties, and I have a nice
Butt that looks good in anything, even naked,
It is such a nice butt, it is round and tight
And firm and pert, it is as nice a butt as
Any could be, and I am happy with it

I Try to Remind Myself That I Am Good Looking

I try to remind myself that I am good looking,
And that I have a nice butt and a nice body
That looks good in a tight summer dress
Or naked when I show my butt in the mirror
To myself, and I have such a nice butt,
And it is mine, my butt, and I like to show it
When I go to the beach and wear a thong
Bikini bottom, and it is almost naked,
Or it really is, for you can see everything

They Would Say It Looked Good, Your Butt

I have a body that is to die for, and a nice face
And you can see me if you look in the mirror
With me, and you would see your own face
There with mine, and you would see your face
Too, and it would be a nice face, just like
Mine, and you would have a nice butt,
For yours is like mine, and you are a woman
With a nice butt, just like me, and you could
Be naked at the beach, and show it in a thong
Bottom bikini, just like me, and it would look
Good, and everyone there would say it looked
Good, for they would notice because it was
Almost naked, and they could see it, they
Could see your bare butt as they could see
My bare butt, at the beach, in a thong bikini,
Really naked because you could see every-
Thing, everything that was there, your butt

You Would Wonder at Such a Nice Butt

I could show you my butt, and you would say
That it was nice, a nice butt, such a nice butt
Naked in the mirror, or in front of you,
For you would be there with me and I would
Turn around and you would see it as I showed
It to you, and you would wonder at such a
Nice butt it could be, there in front of you,
And you would wish you has such nice butt
Unless you did, and you would know
Because mine would be like yours

Just a Bra

There is always something wrong, but there is
Nothing wrong with being a woman,
"It's always something silly like that,"
She said, but a woman is not silly
She can act silly, if it makes her day,
Playing the clown, having fun for her friends,
Laughing and talking and dancing
With no top on, just a bra, because she looks
Good in a bra, just a bra and a cloth skirt
At the party, where she dances with her
Friends, and her friends are laughing
Because she is having so much fun

My Writing for Other Women

I write, especially women, for it is for them
Whom I write, principally, and I want them
To know everything about my nakedness
And sexuality, and my pain and experience
As a woman, like them, a woman like them
But I write to help me, to help myself,
And get stimulation for me, and the
Pleasure and sheer delight of just writing,
Though it is hard, it is difficult, but as I
Experience it, it is very easy, just the words
Rushing up, through me, so quick
I know the meaning only after I have written
It, and this is a thrill, then I discover
What it is all about, and it is a revelation
Each time, each time a revelation about
Myself, what I find inside that is there
So I write for myself, but I write for other
People, other women like me who want
To know about me, what I am all about

Her Niece Is Singing

The child is sleeping soundly, she is dreaming
Of sunshine on a rainy day, there is a
Rainbow: somewhere a child is sleeping,
She may be you, she may be you dreaming
Dreaming of a better day when a better day
Is already here, and she knows it, the child
Knows this, and she sees it in her heart
And her heart lights up, it is bright with her
Visions, her imagination, and she has a great
Imagination, imagining rainbows, in a sunny
Sky on a rainy day, and she is swimming with
Her aunt in a lake, and her aunt is you
So many years ago, with her niece,
And she is singing, her niece is singing,
In bed with her, in the next bed at night
Singing a song that she remembers
From the day before, a day at the beach,
With the rainbow, in the rainy sky

Her Face When She Looked in the Mirror

I was the woman who dreamed she had a
Better face, and she had a better face,
It was on her when she looked in
The mirror already, she had such a
Nice face that she didn't know she had a
Nice face, and she realized it, she found out
She was this beautiful woman
Waking up from her dreams, and seeing
Her face, the face that she had seen
A thousand times, and now she knew
She had it forever, and it was hers

She Had a Nice Smile, and a Nice Laugh

A nice girl whom I gave a cigarette to, on the
Street, on the doorstep of my street, and she
Was cute, with a short houndstooth
Checkered skirt, and several earrings in her]
Ears, and blond hair down to her neck,
And the thick wild thighs of a woman
And it was so satisfying talking to her,
She made my day, right there, that night,
She'd had some drinks but not too many
You could only tell when she said "It was
Great to meet you," and she slurred her words
A little, but not too much, and she had a nice
Smile, and a nice laugh, and I remember her

I Could Put on a Black Romper

I know when summer is coming, I can feel it
In the night stars, the stars at night, as they
Shine in a warm black sky, and I could put on
A black romper, and snap it at my crotch
And feel just like a woman, with a short black
Skirt, as black as the night sky

A Woman with Balls

Tell me I could move my balls in a tight black
Romper, and I would still be a woman,
For a woman can still have balls if she is a
Transgender woman, or she is a transsexual
Or intersex woman, any woman could have
Balls if she chose it, so I choose to have balls
And I am a woman, a woman with balls

That Woman I Can Be

I know what I am, and I know what I can be
I can be a woman, and I am, I am that
Woman, that woman that I can be
It is already I, this woman, this woman is
Already the one that I can be, for she has
Changed to become the woman that she
Could become, and she has become
The one who is I, and I have become her
For I am she, the one she talks to when she
Goes to bed, and when she wakes up
In the morning, to put on her dress
And her summer clothes, so she looks good
For the day, her day with me

So You Can Show Your Legs

Fate has a way of changing things, it is the
Way it would have been before if you hadn't
Changed anything, it is the way it would have
Been if you had been the same, the same
Beautiful woman doing the same things,
Getting naked in the morning to change
Your clothes, put on bra and panties
And put earrings in, and a tight summer dress
Short on the thighs, so you can show
Your legs, your sexy, beautiful legs

Dear Ms. Fantasy

Something to make us happy, Ms. Fantasy,
Something that gives us happiness
Something that brings us to another place
The place where you are, Ms. Fantasy,
In some savanna with the lioness and lion
Smelling the sunflower, in the wide grass
We will give you a flower, the flower you love
We will pick it for you and give it to you
While you open your lips and taste
For the nectar is sweet, of the sunflower
Play us a song, and write us poetry
The song of the sunflower the poet wrote
Ascending its golden clime...
And we will give you gold leaf to cover
Your body so you won't be naked
You will be naked but for the gold leaf
So we can see the shape of your butt,
The shape of your hips, your beautiful
Body, even the crack of your butt
The crack of your butt is beautiful
Everything about you is beautiful

Naked with Other Women, in a Locker Room

Naked with other women, in a locker room,
Checking out each other's body with curious
Eyes, laughing to know we look as cute as
She, the woman drying her breasts with a
Towel, her butt and her pubic hair,
By her vagina, such a cute vagina

The Labor of a Woman

There is always an explanation for who I am,
That woman who presumes that she is
A woman who has a right to be a woman
And I see her, and I say she is this lady
Because I know myself, and I know
I know who she is, this woman, she,
Who this woman is, she is I, she produces,
And she pushes out her text as a woman
Pushes out a child, and it is hers,
It is her labor, this writing, it is the labor
Of a woman, labor of a woman writing
Writing herself, writing her name,
Writing what she is, who she is

The Crack of Her Ass

I have known pleasure, and this night
Knows pleasure, it is the pleasure
Of a woman who has felt herself,
A woman, and it lets her free,
The body sitting in its room, naked,
The body naked touching itself
Pleasure as she knows her hips, waist,
Breasts, the crack of her ass, this
Pleasure, the pleasure of a woman
As she knows herself, as she knows this
Pleasure, deep in her body she knows
This pleasure, and she does, knowing
This pleasure, deep in the night

Public Sex Acts

I have an understanding, an understanding
Of other women, of what women go through,
From the woman who wears the sparkling
Lipstick on the stage of the world,
To the woman that wakes up in the barrio,
The poor district of town, and must wash
At the county well, for her hair is always
Messy in the morning, and I am the
Woman who cleans, and I would be the
Sex worker and the stripper, with my face
Painted white, a tight skirt on my tight butt
And smelling of the first rose of June
And I would be the woman who writes
A book, and reads it at the lectern
In the university hall, reading each word
With care, the manuscript of the book,
Her newest work, that nobody else had read
Except me, for she had shown it to me,
And I had written it, for I was she,
This woman, this universal woman who
Wrote the book, performed the public
Sex acts of the woman who made her body
The alter of a lust goddess who was
Beautiful, and everyone wanted her body
And people have wanted my body,
For I am she, the woman who sold her body

A Symbol of Metamorphosis

A purple butterfly is created as a symbol for a
Woman who has given birth to multiple
Children and lost one or more, and think
This is fitting, for there has been great
Sadness and tragedy in my life, and the
Butterfly is a symbol of metamorphosis
And I have changed into a woman,
I have become a woman, and this is
My metamorphosis, and I will wear the
Purple butterfly on my neck, and say I am
The woman who has suffered tragedy,
The woman who has become a woman

"I Know That You Are a Woman"

I feel inspired sometimes, and I write, I write
Of how I feel inspired, the things inspiring me
The thought of coming out to my mother
In a dress, and saying, "I am a woman,"
And she answers me, "Yes, I know that
You are a woman, and I understand,
It is ok," and if that will ever happen until
She dies and her spirit comes back to me
And she is there, before us, and says she loves
Me, and this has inspired me, to wear a dress
Before my mother, just the thought of it
Before her spirit of the rising, of the dead,
In some haunted hallway that is lovely
Because she is there, and she accepts me

The Woman Who Was Someone Else, but She Was I

I looked at myself, and I was another
Woman, one that looked like me,
With the same lipstick, the same perfume
On her neck, but she had a woman's
Body, down to her wide thighs and hips
And breasts, and she had suffered the
Same things as I, down to the blemishes
On her face, and she was looking at me
And there was sadness in her face,
The same sadness that was in mine,
And I could feel her, I could feel her hurt
The hurt inside, deep inside, and I said,
"I can feel your sadness, I love you,"
And I kissed her, and she said, "I love you,"
And she smiled at me, and she was crying
The same tears that were in my eyes
And she hugged me and kissed my lips
She was I, but she had changed, and become
Another person, with her own being, her

I Can Dream of Laughing with Women

I can have a new dream, of a child,
I can dream of laughing with women,
And understanding each other's body
I could understand another's body,
Another woman's body, just by looking at her
And smiling, and she would smile with me,
That would be enough, we would be
Laughing, we would just be laughing,
There would only be laughter in us
As we looked at each other's body, and smiled
She would speak, and I would listen,
And we would talk together, she and I,
We would understand each other
And we would say the same thing over again
Because that is all we had to say

She Would Recognize Me

Transgender woman hears the music play
She is I, this transgender woman, for I am
A transgender woman, and I know it
And I know when I hear jazz, I can hear
The melody and the beat, the rhythms
And the song I hear, and the song I hear is
Mine, my song, the song of a transgender
Woman, the song I play for myself,
That I wrote for myself, myself,
About the day when I can come out
At my mother's funeral and wear a dress
And read poetry about her, my poetry
About my mother, and remember her
As the wonderful mother that she was
And I can hear the songs they play
On the organ, "Morning Has Broken,"
"Imagine There's No People," and I can
Imagine there are no people, just my mother
And I, and I am reading for my mother
In front of her, at the funeral, her funeral,
A celebration of her of her life
And I would be wearing a dress,
And she would recognize me as a woman

I Have Ripened as a Woman

I have ripened as a woman, I have ripened
Like the language I have used has ripened
The language I use to describe myself,
As the woman I want to be, the woman who is
I, already the one who has filled her dream
Of the ripe fruit ripening, becoming a
Woman, and there has been hard oak
And tragedy, and a summer that has never
Ended, and I will live that summer
With the starlight on my face, in a white
Gauze nightgown at night to hide my shame,
But I have no shame, this night, or in the day,
With the yellow sunlight shining on me,
Shining on me in my bedroom

I Taste Alfalfa Honey

The Lord is my shepherd, she makes me to lie
Down in green pastures, then I wake up
And she is my shepherd, for she makes
Herself a woman, this shepherd who looks
And sees the woman inside me, she is the
Woman who looks at me, and I taste
Alfalfa honey, and it gets stuck on my lips,
And I taste my lips, and they taste of my Lord,
The Lord whose body I have tasted deep
Her body with mine, deep in the night
And she has felt my breasts, and I have felt
Hers, and we have felt each other in the night
Feeling each other's skin, skin of women,
Skin of women deep in our bodies,
Our bodies that run together like the sea
A river running into the sea, she is me
And I have felt her vagina, I have felt
My Lord's vagina, and it was sweet in the
Night, and I have tasted it with my lips
And with my tongue, and we have been
Together, she and I, the Lord, we have been
Together, touching, loving each other's body
In the night, knowing what it was like
To be with the Lord, my Lord, my lover
In heaven, my mistress as I was her mistress,
Even to her butt, her soft butt, as I felt
Her butt, deep in the night, I felt her butt

The Emotions of a Summer Night

I feel the emotions of a summer night, the
Things of the past that come back to me,
Past of another before my memory was there
Memory of a child not yet born, and I
Remember being a child, and the things
I felt, and the things I feel as a woman now
And I feel the feelings a woman feels
The deep emotion, the sorrow for other
People who have lost, long things like
Pets and animals that they love, and I could
The sadness they feel because I know how
It would feel if I lost my pet, it would make
Me cry, I would cry for months, it would feel
Awful, and it would be hard to get over it
And I feel the feelings that a woman feels,
And I feel my body, and I feel my butt
Beneath my tight leather skirt, and I feel
How it feels naked, with my butt showing
In the mirror, my tight butt, my butt
Showing in the mirror with no one there
But me, and I feel that I will live, I will live
As a woman living naked with her butt,
Her butt showing naked in the mirror
With no one there but her, and she knows
She looks good naked, she looks good

When the Sun Is Shining in Summer

To love myself, it is not easy, when there is
So much hardship, and it is hard, and
Painful, but I think of the summer day
And it is nice, and I am there, breathing in
The sun, and I can't remember anything
That is bothering me, just the heat that is
Too much, but it is not too much, for I like it,
And it is the right thing for me... And it is
So easy to love myself when it is a summer
Day, and the sun is shining, I can forget
Anything that doesn't make sense in my life,
I can forget the days when it rains, and it is
Cold, I can forget the accidents that happen
To me, I can go on, being myself and
Loving myself, and it is easy, just snap
My fingers and I am there, in summer,
And summer is here, and everything is all
Right, everything is all right in summer,
And I can go to the beach in a thong
String bikini, and I will look at the other
Women there, and they will look at me
And admire me, they will admire my body,
They will admire my figure with my ass
My butt cheeks sticking out on either side
Of the cloth of the thong, my ass cleft
Visible, and they will say, what a nice body
And they will whisper, but I will hear them

You Like This Woman

Things can happen, but you change them,
And make them something good, and you
Make yourself the woman that you are,
And that is enough, it is enough to be the
Woman that you are, this woman, with her
Body that she likes, body that she is happy
With, and everything about her, and her
Mind, this woman, this woman is you,
And you like her, you like this woman

Sophia, the Name I Chose

I can feel my name, Sophia, it is the name
I gave myself, and it gives me satisfaction
Satisfaction of a woman who has chosen
And I have chosen, chosen my name
And I have chosen to be the woman that
I am, and she is I, this woman, she is I
And it gives me a sense of satisfaction
To breathe my name in the air, and say,
Sophia, it is enough, and when I
Bathe naked under the shower
And clean my body, my face, my ass,
I know that I am clean, I am a clean woman
A clean woman with a name, Sophia
And when I put on a dress or a skirt and top
Over panties and bra, and look at myself
In the mirror, I know that I am good
I am a good woman with a name,
And it is my name, Sophia, the name I chose
And it is enough to make me feel much
Better for whatever hasn't gone right,
It is enough to have the right name,
A nice name, Sophia, and it is mine

I Was a Woman in the Dream

I was the woman who dreamed, and I kept
Dreaming, I dreamed on, feeling the things
That I feel, the moods that came to
My thoughts, and my imagination
Running free, running wild, running
Forever, and I kept dreaming, and I saw
The things I saw as in a vision, and it was
A vision, and yes, I had a vision, and it was
Mine, my vision of the things I always wanted
And I saw them in a dream, and they were
Mine, everything in the dream was mine,
And all I wanted was to be a woman,
And I was a woman in the dream

Tragedy

Tragedy disappears when I write, it becomes
A four-act play in a Greek literature
Anthology, one I read in college or in high
School, and forgot most of what was in it
Except my name, I remember my name,
For I was the heroine of the tragedy,
The Greek tragedy that had my name,
Sophia, the heroine of the play,
The classical play, classic play of all time
That everyone remembers, especially the
Little girls, and the girls who are becoming
Women, for they are like me, I was becoming
A woman, before I became a woman

I Like You

I could look at myself and see a woman I
Liked, and this would be enough, for
Whatever accidents I have had, accidents
That changed me, and if I liked this woman
That would be enough, even if she had
Changed from what she was, and I would look
At her and say, "I like you, you and I, let's
Be together," and we would be together
And I would say that she was good
Because I knew that I was good, and
Everything about her made my day
And if we fought or had an argument or
Disagreed, I would say this was myself,
Someone I had known in dreams,
Someone I had known everywhere,
For she had been with me, for she was

I Could Imagine Myself Buck Naked, and Ask If I Am a Woman

I could imagine myself buck naked, the hair
On my chest, the hair on my navel, the hair
On my balls and on my penis, and ask if I was
A woman, and I would say yes, I am a woman
I have a woman's butt, and a woman's thighs
And a woman's legs, and men and women
Look at them and like them, so I am a woman
A woman with a woman's brain, a woman's
Mind, that thinks about things, thinks about
Things in a different way, more deeply,
Over again, once more, to see the details
That tell everything about the thing
And I have a woman's soul, and a woman's
Heart, that is soft, and big, and hugs
The woman who is near her, or the young
Girl who needs a helping hand, and I have
A face that is like a woman's, I have a
Woman's face, with eyes that are bright
And cheeks that are wide with a smile,
And lips that I put lipstick on that are plush
And soft, and put a kiss on your cheek

Living in Boston as a Transgender Woman

Living in Boston as a woman, a transgender
Woman, it is a small city, not very small,
Rather big, for its size, and I am big,
I am a big woman, 5' 7", big for a woman
And I feel that I fit in this city, I can go
For walks in the various neighborhoods,
And the neighborhoods are such a nice thing
About the city, and I can stop in shops
And have ice cream and coffee, and I like
A double espresso, and ruby chocolate halva,
Or chili, the scent and taste of sesame paste
And the viscous texture, so right for the
Mouth, and I like my friend Hilken's vintage
Clothing shop, I go there and talk to her
And she listens and reassures me and laughs
And I like the basement scene where I used
To go to see underground rock, with all
My friends there, getting high as we used to
Do in the old days, and tapping at my iPhone
To write the reviews I would post on The
Flash Boston, that night, and I like the good
Schools and the hospitals, and the great
Museums where I go to see art, and it gives
Me such a wonderful feeling to see the art
It is a vision state, magically transforming]
Everything into an impressionist painting
And I like sipping a Prana smoothie on the
Greenway on a swinging bench, with

Strawberry and almond butter and dates
And banana, and I like looking at the sun
On the buildings of the skyline, the sky-
Scrapers, that seem so close they are
So tall, and I like the North End's Italian
Restaurants, where I live, and I love
Where I live, it is the hottest neighborhood
In town, in the hottest state, politically,
In the country, and I can use the women's
Bathrooms, and it feels so nice there
And I can dress on the street as I like,
With nobody bothering me, and so many
Admiring the way I look, and commenting
On how nice and pretty a woman I am

My Baby

I can push a thought on the page as a
Woman pushes out a child, and my vagina
Spreads open and the writing comes out,
Thoughts of a woman dreaming, dreaming
Of having a child, and the child is the poetry
She writes, coming out of her vagina
And I spread my legs, and I push my tummy
And the thought comes out, the poetry
Comes out, and this is my child, my child
That I love, my poetry, that comes from me,
As a child comes from a woman, that woman
Me, having a child, my baby, my poetry

The Fine Woman

I could be there, I could go there, it would be
As easy as counting to three, and I would be
There, where I wanted to go... Somewhere,
A place in my own city where I could
Walk down the street and people would look
At me, and say, "My, what a fine woman,
I would like to meet her," and I would
Find a woman, and that woman would find
Me, and we would talk, and we would laugh
Together, just she and I, finding laugher
In each other's eyes, in that special place,
That place that I had found, in
My imagination, that place I found
That gave me what I have needed,
Just to be me, the woman I choose to be

Singing the Top Pop Hits of the Day

I was always the woman who watched TV, but
I didn't watch TV, I listened to the radio
Each day, I would sit at my mother's kitchen
Counter, and hear the top forty played down
Until the song was number one, and I thought
It was the best because it was number one,
And now I am the best because I am number
One, I am the best woman, the best woman
That there is, I am the best woman that there
Is, and I listen to myself on the radio
Because I am a pop star in a red and silver
Gown, singing the top pop hits of the day

She Dreams of Me Dreaming of Her

The heavy emotions of a summer night, I have
Written of them, and the light things
And what it is like to be me, and I have
Written the book on all things being a woman
And the woman does to me what she does
To any woman she dreams of, for she dreams
Of me, she dreams of her dreaming of me
Dreaming of her, and these are the heavy
Emotions, the things she feels, as she dreams
Of herself dreaming of me, and we have
Dreamed of each other at the same time,
Knowing these things in us, the things that
We feel, how we would like to touch each
Other's body, feel our breasts and thighs
And ass, how nice it would feel to touch
Each other's ass, and the crack of our ass

I Am a Forbidden Woman

I am a forbidden woman, I try to bite my heart
Like a woman bending over and eating her
Own pussy… and I get up with the fuck juice
On my lips, it tastes so good, and I do it again
I am a forbidden woman, look at me,
I eat myself out, I eat out my own pussy
Men look at me and they want me,
I tempt them with my body
I am the forbidden woman that tempts men
A harlot that gives them a smile when they
Stand up beside me and say thank you
But I am a virgin, and I don't know any
Men, I have never touched a man, I have
Touched a man in bed, caressed his thighs
And said how beautiful he looked naked
But this was in my imagination, and I am
A chaste virgin, virgin woman, you can't
Touch me but you can think about me,
You can think of me touching your crotch
And making you get hard, but it is only
Me opening my lips and looking at you
I am so beautiful it makes you think
Of performing sex with me, but it will not
Happen, I am a forbidden woman, I am
A forbidden fruit hanging from a vine,
Getting full, and rich, with ripeness
Pendulous on the green jutting vine
With touches of red on my body,

For my body is the fruit, hanging from the
Vine, something you cannot touch
It will never happen because you only see
My lips, touching the pulp of my fruit
The forbidden woman, hanging from
The vine, dropping into the lap
Of a man who sits by me, waiting for me,
Waiting for me to come, and I come,
And it is the ripe fruit wet with its own
Stickiness, the sap of the pulp of my body,
Getting all over you, and you will never
Touch me, you will never touch me, you will
Never touch my body for I am a forbidden
Fruit, a forbidden woman, in the depth
Of the trees, and you will never see me,
You will never even see me, you will just
Find me in your imagination, some image
Of me, some little picture to masturbate on
And you will not forget me, and I will not
Forget you, but you will forget me, and I will
Forget you, for I am a forbidden fruit,
A forbidden woman, the one that shows
Her butt naked in the magazine, the one
You saw so many years ago when you were
Young, and you never forgot me

I Am a Woman Cat

I am as active as my cat, but I am a woman cat
Prancing on the chairs and on the desk
In the students' classroom, putting out
My wand and slapping them on the wrist
When they misbehave, but I misbehave,
For I am a woman cat, and I scratch
The furniture, and I scratch men and women
When they come close to me and breathe
In a way I don't like on me... Speak hard
Words and I will catch you; I will catch you
With my claws, a rat for me to play with
And worry and kill, better than a ball of string
For me to get my dander out, my raw
Aggression, such a curious, awful, wonderful
Thing, such a thing for a woman cat to do

Woman with a Swirling Tattoo

It all comes back to me, the woman with the
Tattoo on her neck, or was it her back?
Memory fades with me, but I remember,
It was the small of her back, the small of the
Left side of her back, right by the butt
Swirling over into her butt and over it
You could see it, above her bare-butt yellow
Bathing suit bottom, and it made me feel sexy,
Wild, she was there, beside me on the beach
On her own striped towel as I was on mine
And she went into the water up to her shins
With her sunglasses on, and I went in
Beside her, and she went back to put her
Sunglasses down, and followed me into the
Water, I have written about this before,
I went out, and she went out, and I waited
To see if she would get her whole body wet
And she did, and I did, and then she put her
Head underwater, and I put mine there
Too, and I swam up beyond her and we both
Came in, and then she lay down on her towel
And I dried myself off and went home'
I wonder what men she has slept with,
Sleeps with, it was so playful what we had
Done together, so much fun, I think she had
As much fun as I did, I am sure she did

I Have Put on Lipstick in the Mirror

I can think back to places I felt so content
I didn't need to leave, and I could go there]
Again, just snap, and I am there, it is that
Easy, sitting in a cottage, eating the
Chocolates my brother had given me
For my birthday, for it was my birthday,
And I went outside so much to have
A cigarette in my tan suede boots,
And they are such nice boots,
And I played music on my iPhone,
Played music on my iPhone all night long,
And everything was all right...
So much happened that winter that was bad,
Things that were unexpected that it made me
Unhappy, and it was so hard to get out of it
I had to think, and I had to write about
Myself as a woman, the woman I am,
And get to know this woman that I am, what
Makes her unhappy, what makes her happy,
The things that she feels, feels all the time,
The thing at the core of her, a love for the
Mind and the human body that studies itself
As a woman studies her lips when she is
Putting on lipstick in the mirror
And I have a body that has studied itself,
And I have put on lipstick in the mirror

I Have Written About a Woman's Pain

I've already done that, I said, created an
Album with no title, The Beatles, Stairway
To Heaven, all white across the ocean
Just me, Sophia, that is all there was
On the cover, my name in bold red print
And I created an album so hardcore
I don't know if anyone will ever read it
Just the raw sexuality of a transgender woman
And I did a book that was all about women
Every single poem, about women or being
A woman, though most of my poems since
Then are about the same, how a woman
Looks at herself naked in the mirror
In bra and panties checking out her butt,
So many poems are about this, exactly this
Same thing, but it is fun, I have so much fun
Doing this that I have no shame, I am not
Ashamed, even when I pull my panties down
And check out the crack of my ass
And write about, or just write about it
Because I didn't do it really, just in
My imagination, which is enough
And I have written about a woman's pain

Short Satin Dress with Panties

It is such a blast; I could dress up in a
Dress every morning, or a skirt and top or a
Romper, or a jumpsuit or white bicycle pants
With a short satin dress that would be too
Short to wear without them, it would show
My panties, and I wouldn't be ashamed
But I couldn't go out like that, people would
See me and they would say something,
Or they would look at me askance
Through the corner of their eye,
And I would know it isn't right
Or I could be at a party where everyone
Knew me, it would be all right to wear
Indoors with the panties showing

I Am a Woman Who Tasted the Fruit

The African beat starts, and I think of an
African woman, full breasts bare naked,
As she looks at the noonday sun
I could be that woman, running with a
Jug of water on my neck, just the sun and I
Grain in its sacks, waiting to be ground,
I could think of being the white woman
That I am, sipping a cup of coffee
In my living room, playing the African music
Be happy I have a body that is healthy,
That looks good as I put on a leather skirt
And a leopard skin top, and I felt like a
A woman inside, a woman that
Climbs the vines of the trees with the fruit
Hanging from them, and I could be content
Eating the fruit, the hanging fruit,
Forbidden only to me, I am a woman who
Tasted the fruit, and found it was
What she had wanted, the taste
Of a fine night out in a black gown,
A glittering black gown, tight on my waist,
Under the stars and the marquees,
And I was a star, I was one of the stars

I Look Like a Woman

It is a woman's body that I have, though you
May say that it looks like a man's,
It is something I wear on me with fashion
Like spring fashion going into summer

If you look at my body naked, you will see
The solid contours of a woman
With the look in her face of a woman,
For I look like a woman, this I know

I can wear a bra and panties and you couldn't
Tell I wasn't born a woman, a biological
Woman, my butt is soft and round
And firm and hard, and it is a nice penis

With balls that are big but just the right
Size, and I look like a woman, yes, I know
I know that I look like a woman,
It is written in my face, that I am a woman

A Beautiful Cunt

I have been everywhere, I have touched the
Gold skirt of the woman I liked, and lifted
The hem and touched her cunt, and it was
A beautiful cunt, full of hair, pubic hair
That made me laugh with laughter
It was so curly and short, black hair,
Just like the hair she had on her head
And it was wonderful, and I wondered
If I could be a woman like her, with a pussy
A nice pussy full of hair, just like hers

I Am a Naked Tahitian Woman

Where do we go from here? Gauguin could
Ask the question with the naked Tahitian
Women in the painting, and I am a
Naked Tahitian woman, with my breasts
Protruding out, my nice, wonderful, full
Breasts, and my brown skin, and my cunt
With its straight black hair around it,
Such a nice cunt, betrayed to the morning air
And I have lips of plum and almond,
And I am a nice woman, you could touch me
And I would smile, and that is where we go
From here, smiling, and I am smiling at you
And I am smiling with you, for we smile
Together, you and I, and us, we smile for us

A Woman Thinks About Herself

You live with an ache, and you understand
A woman's pain, an ache that doesn't let you
Go, unless you say, this is the way it was
Meant to be, and it is all right... And it is all
Right, and the ache fades, it is just another
Thing in life that goes away, the ache in the
Pit of your stomach, in your body, the body
Of a woman, yours, your body, a woman's
Body, recovering, rehabilitating, becoming
What it was, the body of a woman that is all
Right, with her breasts on right, her pubic
Hair over her vagina, her ass with the cleft
Of her ass, her legs, her hips, and her thighs,
And her face, the pretty face of a woman
And it is yours, you are that woman,
And you are free of ache because you have
Let your existence speak, the existence of
A woman, and you exist, this woman, you,
You exist, and you know you exist

My Body in the Shape of a Butterfly

My eyes open wide, I can't believe what I see
Before me, my whole body in the shape
Of a butterfly, a purple butterfly
With indigo markings, and it is so wonderful,
It is wonder, and it is mine, my body
My soul, in my eyes before me
And this is my body whole, naked
With every part of me showing,
My butt, my thighs, my legs, my flat breasts,
For my breasts are flat for a woman,
It is a thing that I had dyed there
By an artist, the purple tattoo, and I can feel it
In my fingers as I hold it and let it go
And it is my body fluttering to a flower
To find the nectar inside, the nectar that
Keeps me beautiful, and gorgeous, and
Lovely to behold, and behold, I am
There, flying into the summer,
Wings spread wide, on extended wing
Under the sky blistering with sun

Under the Hot Spray

I could be with other women naked, checking
Out each other's butts and each other's
Pussies, and they would check out my balls
And my penis, and see that I was a
Handsome woman, and we might be in the
Shower in the locker room, under the hot
Spray, and we would spray each other
With the spray, laughing and laughing
And looking at each other's bodies,
Each other's cunts and penises,
The women who had penises, and the
Ones who didn't, but cunts, nice cuts
With curly and short black hairs around them

She Looks in the Mirror at Her Ass

I have been inside the woman that I am, and I
Have found her nice, this nice woman that
I am, and she has found that she is sweet
When I looked at her, with a nice face
And nice lips when she puts lipstick on,
And a nice mind, she has a nice mind
And she is a nice person, and she has a nice
Body, her body is as nice as it can be
And when she looks in the mirror she says
"I have a nice ass," for she looks in it
Backwards, and sees her ass...
And when she looks in it backwards, she says,
"I have a nice crack in my ass," for she has
A nice crack in her ass, and she knows
For she has seen it when she looked in the
Mirror backwards, and saw her ass

"Your Whole Body Is Nice"

The only way to feel better is to accept
Yourself, and be the woman you love
She will guide you; she will help you,
She will give you what you need
And I have been that woman, I have been
Myself, giving me the things that I need
Looking me in the face in the mirror
And saying, "I love you," and she has been
There for me, saying things that make me
Feel good, giving me things, telling me that
I am all right, that I look beautiful in a green
Dress, or a blue dress in the night,
Or naked, with the crack of my ass visible,
And she has said, "You have such a nice
Big, soft, round ass," and I let her touch
My ass, and she said it felt nice, "You have
Such a nice ass, and a nice crack in your ass,
Your whole body is nice, such a nice body
You have", and it was her body because
She was I; she was I speaking to myself
Saying what a nice body I have

Every Woman Has an Ass

I know everything, everything about being
A woman, and it makes me a woman
I have written about it, and it gives me
Knowledge, knowledge of a woman's body
That I could not have unless I write
And it gives me knowledge of a woman's
Feelings, and a woman's thoughts,
Women's thoughts as look in the mirror
And check out their ass, their beautiful ass
Turned to the glass at just the right angle,
And every woman has an ass, an ass that is
Nice, and a nice crack in the ass,
And her whole ass is nice, down to the
Butt cheeks on either side, and the thighs
And her hips, she has such nice hips,
Every woman has nice hips, and I know about
These hips because I have written about them

Girlfriend

Thoughts from a past, a long time ago
A woman I used to know, if you could say
I knew her, she was an acquaintance
But I liked her, I even really loved her
And I missed her when she was away
And she used to come and talk to me
When I was on my doorstep, and she was
Was walking on by, and we used to laugh
And chat with each other for a long time
Someone said she liked a woman, that she
Was a lesbian, that she was gay, and that she
Had a partner whom she lived with
And I even met the partner though I thought
It was just a friend, and maybe she was
It could be just a rumor they were girlfriends
She said she had a long-distance boyfriend
And that she was going to spend the weekend
Once, and I said I wanted to be your boy-
Friend, and she said she had one, but I was
Sad, I really wanted her for a girlfriend

I Need Me

I am all set for life, I only need me, I don't
Need another woman, I am my only
Woman, and it has been so long for me,
But I only get stronger, I only get
Stronger for myself, the only woman
I need, and I need a woman, I need me

They Are Proud

If your dreams defeat you, you rise again
And you are in the women's locker room,
And you are the only transgender woman
There, or maybe there is another, and she is
Your friend, and you are there together,
And these other women who are there,
You see them stripping to panties and bra,
Coming in from swimming or the gym
With sweat on their bodies, they see you,
They are proud of you that you have come,
And you take off your clothes and they see
You and you are as pretty and cute and
Lovely and beautiful and sexy as they feel
That they are, being in the shower with you,
And they are proud of this, they are naked
Too, for they have taken off their clothes
And you are in the shower, and you are
Comparing each other's bodies, how they look
In the water, showering over them, and she
Notices your butt, one of them, and she
Says, what a nice ass, and she says I have
A nice ass too, look at it, so you look it with
Curious eyes, she is right, she has a nice ass,
She says, look at the pubic hair on my cunt,
And you look at it, and it is nice, and you
Smile, for you are in the women's locker
Room, with the other women, and they are
Proud of you, and this is your dream

Even When I Am in Bra and Panties Naked

I never got so big that I didn't often feel small
I am small if you compare me to a man,
But I am tall if you compare me to a woman
Another woman, I am a transgender woman
So I would desire to be compared to
Another woman, and if you compare
My breast size, they are small, for my breasts
Are flat, I never had them done, had a boob
Job, as so many other transgender women
Do, though I have tried estrogen, but I
Changed my mind, twice, and it was a
Difficult choice, a difficult decision
And I am a small poet like Emily Dickinson
Or Sappho, nobody reads me, or few,
But I have a nice face, and a nice ass
And nice thighs and nice legs
And this makes me proud, so I am proud
To be a woman, I am proud to be this woman

The Woman Who Listens

The woman who listens, the woman who
Wears blackberry lipstick because she likes
Berry shades, she likes berry shades of
Lipstick because she thinks they look good
On her, they make her look mysterious
And dark, a dark woman who is mysterious
And listens, listens to you, as she tells you
The story of her darkness, and you ask
Questions, and she listens very carefully
To your questions, and she answers them,
About how she became this woman that she
Is, this woman who became, this woman who
Opens her lips and sings at the slightest
Motivation, the motivation to show her body
Buck naked, in bra and black leather thong
Panties because she is sexy, because she is
A sexy woman who likes to show off her body

The Crowned Queen

There is some forward motion, and I move it
I move it like a woman, I move it like a woman
Should, bending my legs and putting
My butt cheeks out for a man to push into it
And my anus is mysterious and dark
Pushed out like that for all to see by the
Camera, and I am docile and submissive
But I shove my mouth on his manhood
And I am the active woman, looking like
The crowned queen, but without any clothes

I Made a Decision About My Gender

There are always things that are changing,
The mind changes, it makes a different
Decision, and I made a decision about
My gender, I decided I was a woman
So I changed my name to Sophia,
And became a woman, and I put on bra
And panties, thong panties because I like
To show my butt, in tight skirts, miniskirts
That are short on the thigh because I like
To show my thighs, I have nice thighs,
And I don't mind if men see my panties
Between my legs though I try to cover them
Up my keeping my knees together

This Is My Day at the Beach

A day at the beach, in a thong bikini, and I am
The envy of everyone there with my cheeks
Hanging out of my bottom, my butt cheeks
That look so nice on my ass because I have
A nice ass, and I have a nice chest so
My bandeau top looks good, my leopard skin
Bandeau top, and I go to get an ice cream
Cone, and a black man harasses me,
But I don't care, but I do, and I talk back
To him, and he is obnoxious, so I tell him
To leave, and he leaves, and this is my day
At the beach, except there were three nice
Young women who talked to me afterwards,
And I went swimming in the water
And I like the sparkling sea, how it looks
On me, as I dive and splash in the waves,
Then I come out, and dry myself off,
And listen to my iPhone, and go back
In the water again, and then I pack
My backpack with my towel, and I go home

I Buried Myself in My Breasts

I buried myself in my breasts, full mammary
Things, though they are quite flat for a
Woman, they are my breasts, and they are
Mine, and they are a woman's breasts
Because I am a woman, and I buried myself
In my breasts just to find the time to write
My poetry, just to find the time to write
My name, which is my poetry, my poetry
Is my name, and my name is lady mother
Of the sky, with her angel high, and I get
In a trance with my love, and just write on
My love for sure images, my love of language,
My love for the breasts of the body, and the
Body's curves, the curve of the hips,
The curve of the thighs, the neck the face
But most of all the ass, the curve of the ass
And I write about the curve of the ass

A Woman in a Black Leather Garter Belt

I feel the energy active inside me, building,
And I have become a mistress to a mistress
Mistress to me building where I sleep,
Giving sharp orders with a whip on the wrist
A leather whip, with the crack of mine
That is of a woman in a leather garter belt
And black leather thong panties and a
Bra without cups to hide my nipple buds,
And I have been powerful, as mascara
Ran down my face with my salt sweat
And tears, for I have laughed, and I have
Felt the energy run down me as I beat
A man to bloody shreds, and he cried
And thanked me afterward for all I did
And he was naked, and I liked his butt,
So I touched it and grabbed it with the
Palms of my hands, and thanked him for
Being my obedient servant and slave

Black Leather Underwear

There are so many people I don't like, and I
Don't like them, and it makes me mad
To think about them, so I think of something
Else, I think of me, and how I could become
Better, and forget the anger in my heart
And that would be nice, I would just think
Of the one I am, growing, being the one I am,
Forgetting the ones who make me angry,
And dressing up, wearing black leather
Underwear, a bra, and a black leather
Thong bikini, and that would be enough,
It would be enough to be me, looking in the
Mirror or being photographed for a B & D
Magazine, the one with black eyeshadow,
Or purple eye shadow, and black mascara
And black lipstick, and this would be me,
How I know myself, and I would be happy

Statue of Me as a Woman

I have achieved great moments, but I have lost
Great moments in the stampede, the
Stampede where the horses run, and every-
Thing is in the dust, and my poetry is in the
Dust, and it is stamped over, but I have risen
Again, and I have walked, and I have run,
I have run as a great horse running across
The plain... And I have been that great horse,
That great horse running, putting one hoof
In front of the other, pushing as hard as I can,
And running across the plain again
And I have lost all my pride as a woman,
But I have regained it, this naked woman
In all the glory of her naked body,
Standing as a great statue in the city
With my breasts standing proud in the square
And my pubic hair has been glorious,
As the glorious pubic hair of a woman,
And my vulva has been plump, in the bronze,
And my behind has been full and rich
As a woman's is, on the statue, in the city,
In the square, and I have been there as a
Woman, the woman you have seen,
The woman I have seen when I walked there

Dominatrix in the Living Room

I am only interested in men physically, but
That could change, or I like men if they like
Me, and they are nice people, and I would
Like them, and I would start to have some
Kind of feelings for them, and even be
Submissive, men like that, but I like to be
The domineering dominatrix in the living
Room or the bedroom with a whip
Smashing their butts with lashes
My eyelashes batting with mascara
And I would grab their butts in a fearsome
Passion, and say I love you, I love your butt

She Is I

It is just me, being who I am, this one who
Opens my lips, and speaks from another
Place, opening her lips and singing,
A song of a place, her place, in the home,
In the kitchen, in the living room, in the
Bedroom, and this is what she does
And she sings of her long day, of cooking
And ironing and scrubbing the kitchen floor,
And putting the children to bed and changing
Their diapers, and feeding them breakfast
In the morning so they can go to school
And changing the sheets, so she can rest,
And having sex with her husband, she is I,
And this is I, this is what I have done,
As a woman, as the woman I am

A Woman Moist

A peck puts me out, it is the heat in my old
Age that makes me dry, but I am as wet
As a woman warm between the legs,
And my panties get wet, they get wet
And I am a woman moist, and I am thinking
About my butt and how hot it is, and I would
Like to wear hot pants and go in the sun
I would like to walk on the streets of summer
In hot pants almost nude, showing my butt

Black Long-Sleeve Teddy

The Black woman sings, she sings of love,
Of heartache, and she is a woman of soul
And you can hear her when she sings,
For she sings loud, but it is soft,
Soft as a feather pillow on your bed
And I have lain on that pillow,
Dreaming of a black long-sleeve see-through
Mesh teddy, that I could wear, on that bed
If only I could buy it, and I would, and I
Almost would, if I could wear it anywhere
Outside my bedroom, but it would be so nice
Just to wear it in my bedroom, as the stars
Shone in the window, and the Black woman
Sang, so sweet of love and heartache,
The woman with soul, on the radio

The Woman of Death Finds You, and She Dresses You in a Black Lace Teddy

The long journey to death, where the woman
Of death finds you, and she dresses you in a
Black lace teddy, and you look fine, the
Woman ready for death, and death finds you,
And she puts her hands on your cheeks,
And she kisses your cheeks, and you are ready
For death, and you look so fine in your black
Lace teddy, and you take one last glance
In the mirror, and you don't want to go,
So you stay, in your bedroom, in your black
Lace teddy, looking so fine, and you look
Once again in the mirror and you kiss your
Mouth with your lipstick lips, and you stay

I Went as Far as I Could

I went as far as I could in being a woman,
And then I went more, I went further
Into being a woman than I ever could possibly
Have before, and the sun shone on me
And I just spoke whatever I wanted to have
Said, and it was mine, my words were mine,
The words of a woman mine, and I could
Put on panties in the night and say, this is I
A semi-naked woman, but they were thong
Panties so I was naked because you could
See my butt, and it was a nice butt
With the butt cheeks sticking out on each
Side of the thong, the strip that goes up
My asshole, my anus, and I would check
Myself out, check myself out in the mirror
And say how nice I am, what a nice woman

- June 25, 2022

Sophia Marshall is a perceptual poet, characterized by her treatment of the senses. She has been compared to e.e. cummings, Gerard Manley Hopkins, Emily Dickinson, and Sappho. She is a credentialed journalist and music critic, as well as a poet, with credits in several jazz journals and other music publications, and she has published letters on politics in *The Boston Phoenix*. She has a blog, The Flash Boston (theflashboston.com), covering Boston music and culture. She is a transgender woman. She lives in Boston.

Cover text: Bodoni 72
Body text: Didot

Design: Sophia Marshall
Author photo: Tiffany Nguyen

Made in the USA
Middletown, DE
10 July 2022